A Jennifer Lopez Short Narrative & True Story

I have no fear of depths and a great fear of shallow living.
~Anais Nin

DEDICATION:

TO MY HUSBAND, FELIPE.
YOUR WORK ETHIC, DEVOTION TO FAMILY
& TO LIVING WITH AN HONEST PURPOSE
ARE TRUE WEALTH.

~

TO MEXICO, ANDRES MANUEL LOPEZ
OBRADOR [AMLOve].
YOU ARE A SHINING STAR IN THE NIGHT
SKY…
A CULTURE WHO MUST BECOME VALUED
FOR ITS TRUE WORTH AND BRILLIANCE.

Wealth is the ability to fully experience life.
~Henry David Thoreau

To know wealth, is to understand when you have something so valuable—no amount of money in the world could ever buy it. That is riches.
~Unknown

Welcome inside these precious brief
pages.
So glad you came…
inside my heart,
inside my true story.

Before we begin, please look around you.

Inhale a deep breath of gratitude for all the good that's come to you in your life... even in the smallest of ways.
Exhale any vestiges of doubt or discouragement away.
Get ready.
...ready to think differently.
Open your heart.
Open your mind.
You may find that you just opened up a whole new way of life.

Our world is not shaped by those who think similarly,
but by those who dare to think differently.
~Rashida Rowe

I have been thinking about the idea of wealth lately.

What is WEALTH?

I have a true story to share—whose impact may remain long after you finish reading its truth. But before I tell you. I want to briefly explore the word 'wealth'.

WEALTH is common nomenclature in our society today. It is a word used to discuss high attainment. Why do some individuals seem almost…programed to desire monetary wealth… to the extent that their lives revolve entirely around striving to attain it?

Having lived in the heart of other Spanish-speaking countries for lengthy periods throughout my life, I've noticed significant cultural differences in how the meaning of wealth is perceived.

In the United States [which comprises only a portion of North America—or Las Americas], there is an almost blinding intensity among the current generation, mentally driving and inundating the aspiration for material gain. There's also a significant mainstream perception regarding the happiness, status & the freedom that monetary wealth brings.

The perception I mention, seems to result in a craving for absolute attainment of all that matters to meet and exceed one's human 'needs'.

Once you've 'arrived at wealth,' you've 'attained true freedom & status' —as well as the power that comes with it. Doesn't this sound like the general consensus of what wealth attainment represents in our society today? Is there anything wrong with this, when the claims of wealth (based on this premise) tout the promise of a worry-free life and an ability to access the once, previously inaccessible?

Every human being deserves the right to feel a sense of personal freedom and the ability to enjoy a life of fruition, especially when dedicated efforts and work create those desired results. Essentially then, many in our society would make this assertion: monetary wealth is the freedom that represents the 'American Dream.'

What about in other societies? Is there a different kind of wealth?

* * *

Personally, I can't purport extraordinary expertise in the area of monetary wealth attainment. HOWEVER, I have a very "THINK DIFFER-ENT" definition of the word WEALTH. There are some undeniably important things I've learned from many years of personal experience, as well as being a profound observer in life.

These experiences, I suppose- allow me some

sort of claim to share my understanding of wealth– as I see it.

Come on, grab a 'Hellooote Sabroso' here, sit back in your seat, share this little story and enjoy a brief life-changing moment to think differently.

(ps-Elotes & Esquites are super delicioso!)

You'll soon get what I mean by me 'staking my own small claim' on such a 'BIG' word as wealth.

* * *

Okay, so- I've known many: acquaintances, close family friends & others- who've attained extraordinary monetary freedom by revering it as the primary goal at the forefront of their life's purpose. I've lived, studied and worked among the 'wealthiest' of individuals and seen first hand the unlimited supply of material possessions, activities and social notoriety that go along with this monetary wealth.

I've also lived abroad for lengthy amounts of time- among the 'poorest' of the poor; those whose homes could only be called such—for the mere fact that they were surrounded by loved ones—but certainly not for a solid structure or set of conveniences it afforded them.

When I was younger, I couldn't fully grasp the reasons I felt significantly deeper connections in life, with people I met from various cultures outside of the U.S. and even in some small farming communities within the states. These friends, led family-centered lives of simplicity where monetary wealth was not the focus. Almost without exception, they exuded MUCH more joy and innate freedom of self-expression —compared to others I knew— who had everything the material world could offer.

These family-centered & culturally in-tune individuals, both at home & abroad were often self-educated, yet their knowledge, inner-wisdom and willingness to connect deeply with life in general seemed to surpass that of many conventionally educated people I knew.

It was different, hard to explain, and seemed backwards to me…having grown up entrenched in a culture where the predominant focus was on keeping up with social expectation, 'fitting in' and observing the need for others to do whatever it took to always had the latest, newest of whatever was said to be cool or 'important'.

* * *

I just FELT something beautifully connected

within the culture of simplicity.

As time passed, it slowly came to light for me: my hard-working friends of various cultures, small communities or modest livings–had a pre-served innocence and their freedom of self-ex-pression came from dedication and devotion to some higher purpose, work ethic with goals di-rected at making a difference, forging genuine connections, helping others even when you bare-ly had enough to help yourself, devotion to fami-ly-centered lives, and to self-less expressions.

The beauty—despite tremendous poverty, the supply for essential needs was often found through communal sharing and caring. There ex-ists an almost childlike nature in the innocence of the people as well—the appreciation for sim-ple joys when the work is done.

There was no air of pretension because their val-ues innately placed authority upon living more deeply-centered lives, without dependence on extraneous "things" for happiness— lives lacking concern over other people's perceptions of them.

It was making sense.

On the contrary, when I passed time with others I knew well, those from more wealth-driven backgrounds (who were also a significant part of my life due to work, school etc.)–time spent was extraordinarily different. Not just different–it lacked that natural simple joy, and complete freedom of self-expression. So often, I observed my friends conversations, listening as they seemed strained, feeling the need to convince others, they (even their own kids) were doing the right things or better things. Conversations seemed—more… trivial.

Sometimes there were huge looming clouds of worry over drama of something easily fixed with a bit more self-awareness. Concern for what others thought, talk of appearances, the latest material items–even one's ability to 'throw weight around' with a particular individual due to 'who' they were; Everything felt more forced, very surface-centered and STIFLED.

Exhausting

It may not be something you are aware of on a conscious level…but here's some food for thought. When you are around anyone who is unimpressed by the mere material—and interested in YOU for the genuine nature you allow yourself to express around them—they gravitate to that expression of the pure and innocent mind. WHY? It takes us to the place of who we are–most naturally.

To NOT be impressed with the superficial, socially confining–you know… to THINK DIFFERENTLY– maybe that's what we all naturally want.

OKAY, WELL, WE'VE ARRIVED…

A MAGNIFICENT & TRUE STORY~

HOW FINDING MY DEFINITION OF WEALTH CHANGED MY LIFE!

The first time FULL UNDERSTANDING of everything above made its impact on me was when I decided to move to the heart of a small

Mexican village to teach, in between college and grad school. I call it the "Real Mexico."

I walked down the same cobble-stone street every morning heading to my class of English as a Second Language students. Each morning I saw this one man, working on the street–making repairs on that old stone road. He was literally down so deep inside the ground, that only his head and a bit of his upper shoulders and arms were visible. He was surrounded on all sides by the cobbled stones he had piled up as he removed them to make repairs.

Every day when I passed, he stopped his work, looked up with a kind smile and sweat dripping off his brows, and said to me (and other passers-by), "Hola, ¿Cómo están Ustedes? Qué día más bonito hoy, ¿No?"

[Hello you all, what a beautiful day today, true?]

I often ran a bit late to class because all I could think was: this man needed 'un aguita de melon' from a cart not far away—and I'd get it for him.

The other passers-by would reply kindly & carry on. This happened each day and after passing him and occasionally setting down this fresh melon juice, I would think: here was this ONE incredibly hard-working man with no help whatsoever in his challenging job and more than enough for ten men to complete (especially lacking the modern tools or methods necessary for a more speedy repair). He could easily feel overwhelmed, defeated and negative from the cumbersome nature of his work. But this man instead—chose to look at life for the beauty the day held—everyday.

I could sense this within him. There was an effort to push beyond and keep striving, despite the adversity of his work situation. There seemed something else…as an observer…yet whatever it was, didn't prevent him from giving his work all he had and more!

Little did I know, how much more there was to his story.

The *best* is yet to come.

Our morning greetings continued and some brief conversations even began. I learned his name: Alberto—and remember feeling grateful to hear a bit about his children. The joy and pride he had for them made his face light up. I was most appreciative of the opportunity to have those brief moments of interaction and the exchange of genuinely kind exchanges of moral support, before continuing our long days. He may have been a stranger, but we grew in respect for one another—as humans striving to make the best of life. I continued to pass by on the narrow side-brim of the street on my walk home at the end of each day and bid him a good evening, as he was cleaning up at sunset.

* * *

The completion of my language classes was near and I was coming upon the end of my time there in REAL Mexico. It happened, that Alberto's work on the road was also coming to completion around the same time. I could see the transformation and how he'd managed—all on his own

—to reestablish the cobble stone street, so it could be utilised one again.

On my final day of class, I was later than usual in my classroom finishing up the last paperwork.

I had not seen Alberto that morning, since the director of my teaching program offered to take me for an early coffee before work and drive me to my final classes.

When finishing up that evening, the though occurred to me, I might not be able to say goodby to Alberto, especially with the remaining work I had to complete for my students and in order to close up the classroom.

On my final walk toward what had become my home-away-from-home; my thoughts overwhelmed me over the experience with my receptive students and their enthusiasm about learning. As I neared the cobblestone street, my heart hoped against reality. Sun had set and was now into twilight. Seeing Alberto to say goodbye was unlikely at best.

Maybe this was the way it was meant to be. Goodbyes were never a happy thing and everything about our brief but meaningful exchanges had been happy.

Turning the corner, I noticed the repaired cobblestone. It looks so pretty. *All things culminate.*

At that moment, I noticed some movement in a corner where two buildings met—leaving a slightly larger space on the walking rim. It was a triangular area where I'd often noticed people congregate, all squished together, catching some shade and chatting on my way into work.

Well, there he was, on that corner. Alberto, hunched over, worked at piling up some salvaged cobblestone in neat piles…such precision and meticulousness.

My heart smiled—he was still there. He stood, examining this little work site. I headed toward him and spoke up. Saying his name felt good—

knowing I'd been afforded this final opportunity to express my happiness at having been able to observe his example of what I considered true humanity. Commenting on the beautiful work he had done to preserve the integrity of this long historical road, we stood smiling at the antiquity made new.

Alberto was a middle aged man and up close the deep-set lines in his sun browned face seemed to show forth the wisdom of a full life lived.

After informing him about the conclusion of my classes, we stood smiling and chatting over the circumstance that we had both reached the end of our own individual projects in the same time frame. *How interesting was life.*

We continued visiting, and I asked of his family, remembering the day he'd beamed at sharing the love for his children. He spoke freely of his children (all 8 of them) and his deep love for his wife. I was taken a-back for a moment when he asked me if I would have the time or interest in meeting his family, since he was also on his way home. He assured me his family would appreciate my visit, explaining that his oldest daughter, 12 years of age was making rice tonight. I asked where they lived. He pointed. It was up the nearest mountain.

Alberto said it would be a long walk for me, so he would pay for a small cabby to take us up. Without belaboring the point that many of you might rightfully be thinking….

Whaaaat??

How naïve could I be to travel with a stranger up a mountain to "meet his family" and dine with them when I knew nothing about them—or even if there really was a family. I will simply leave it at this: I had not a single doubt propelled further by a keen intuition that I was meant to go. There was a strong sense of peace that accompanied me up the mountain with Alberto. So, though it could have been an unwise decision in some cases, I knew for me, in my circumstance AND in my gut… it was more than ok.

* * *

When we arrived at the top of the mountain, Alberto helped me down from the cabby, pulled out some pesos and paid the man. I froze there on the dirt road, as the cabby pulled over to park a short way up. There was no house; there were no houses at all. It took me quite a moment to compose myself—emotions had risen up within me and so had tears, flooding my eyes as I worked to suppress them. I turned, bent down and adjusted my shoe…trying to remove my own selfish emotion from such a selfless situation.

This man, Alberto—just paid for me to ride up to his home. It was likely something he never ever did for himself and was probably a huge chunk from his earnings. My mind full and processing…

There in front of me was a teeny village of maybe 30 families whose homes were made of nothing more than tarps, plastic, cardboard and a few wooden boards here or there to hold up the corners. There were no real streets and the electricity was just one long wire that ran zigzagging from tattered post to post.

What I can tell you now: these were real homes, meeting the most fundamental of all needs—completely unsullied love.

* * *

The family came out, lifting a dark tarp and ducking under. The children ran to their father's welcoming arms. Then their precious faces looked at me, smiling and came to warmly greet this stranger that their papa had brought home for a visit. They were jumping and happy!

I felt enveloped in a tremendous warmth immediately, the kind few in life express this authentically.

A truly rich man is one whose children run into his arms when his hands are empty.

~Unknown

I was ushered into their home through a side door made of three slats of wood and a board nailed diagonally across them.

I entered a small room—the home in its entirety. There, a sheet of corrugated opaque plastic created a ceiling that covered only a portion of the room where 6 of the young children returned to sit on one large bed, positioned in the corner, directly on the dusty ground. Practically up against the bed was an old stove; it was the kind you'd see thrown on a curb for garbage day in many parts of the Unites States. Above it, hanging from a wire, was one light—their only light. That was it, everything they had. I sat down on a crate in the center of the home and got to visit with the children.

After learning their names, we began to sing a

Spanish song they were teaching me...all the while...I was being warmly hugged by two of the little ones (Guadalupe and Adolfo) who'd come over off the bed to clutch my legs and rest their heads on my knees with the most endearing warmth. They looked up at me as we all sang and laughed—their huge chocolate coloured eyes smiled into my soul.

The eldest daughter, 12 year old, Blanca-Estrella (White Star) lovingly glanced at me as she stirred the rice on the stove. I could smell lovely herbs and a gentle spice, as it began to waft through the air around us. I stood up and asked Blanca-Estrella if she needed any help and she responded immediately, coming over and placing her baby sister Esperanza (meaning: Hope) in my arms while she finished the rice. She had been holding her the entire time...

Plop. There I was... holding this tiny, cherub-faced, easy-going little one; my entire heart melting with her there in my arms.

That initial feeling I had upon arriving and seeing the village, rushed through me again. I struggled tremendously, to hold back a massive flood of tears for the many thoughts passing through my mind. The answer seemed obvious.

I asked Alberto if he would mind me walking just outside their home to look at the beautiful view with the baby, for a moment. He assured me that was fine. I heard him quietly tell the children to stay inside and give me a moment.

As I walked out, I noticed their bathroom area, not far from the home. It was just a couple of deep holes in the ground. I had to remind myself that at least they had electricity and a small community well for some water supply.

The tears came rushing down anyway and I stood there holding Esperanza, with my back to the family home. I walked a bit further, quietly bouncing the baby and trying to hide this wave of uncontrollable emotion.

While holding la hermosa pequeñita, I tried with every power in me to compose myself for the sake of this most precious family that had graciously welcomed me: a stranger into their home. I had arrived at the edge of the terrain, before it became bramble. Looking out over the mountainside, the town below appeared in my sight and I witnessed the most breath-taking view I had seen during my entire time there in REAL MEXICO.

The tears began to pour out quietly but forcefully as my body quivered and I felt the hermosa pequeñita grip one of my fingers with her entire hand. She was such an incredible little one.

Feeling a hand on my shoulder, I turned to realise Alberto had come over to check on us.

I will never in my life forget what he said, upon seeing my face swollen from the quiet sobs and my body trembling.

"No llores por favor, ni temes Jennie, mira lo que hay. Este es valor puro- el valor más verdadero."

[Don't cry, please, neither fear Jennie, look at what there IS…pure wealth- the truest wealth.]

That was all he said and it was clear—beyond a shadow of a doubt that we had both communicated deeply with so few words. He had already known I cared and he wanted me to understand they were more than ok, they were happy.

Alberto taught me something that has remained

with me from that point on. True wealth comes from within and can be ours, despite even the seemingly worst of circumstances.

* * *

I found out during dinner that Alberto's wife—the mother of these 8 precious children, had passed on 3 months earlier from a terminal illness and Blanca-Estrella stopped attending school to care for the younger ones while her papa worked. Here they were, making every moment count with love and gratitude, despite the absolute tragedy they had just passed through.

Tears or remorse for them were selfish, not to mention—a way of bringing their uplifted energy down. This sweet family was sharing and showing me their STRENGTH of spirit, despite the tribulation they'd recently faced. Their understanding of True Wealth…most certainly was a higher, deeper grasping of the truths in life, a lesson some of the most educated, well-read and wealthy individuals I knew were nowhere near comprehending.

* * *

Although the story continued thereafter, in some small way...I will leave it with you there and add only this to conclude: after awakening to the realization that Alberto had spent money he didn't have to spend...on the cabby (even having the gentleman wait)—in order to make it easier for me; it was clear he understood my time there was ending. Without hesitation, in his value for humanity—he wanted to live in the moment and share the most important part of his life with someone who he sensed in his heart sincerely cared. He could have much more easily just said his goodbye and had the fond memory of our daily greetings in his heart.

He knew the only way I would be able to meet his family was to go there, since there were so many of them. He refused to accept my paying him back for the cabby ride so I quickly left the money in between some bowls piled on one side of the stove when he went to retrieve the cabby for me. He wasn't looking for anything from me. He didn't even have an address. He knew this was most probably the last time I'd ever see him and he wanted to have his children meet a person who had just maybe brought a tiny light into his struggling days.

I hugged each precious child goodbye. I will tell you I did cry. It was the third time. But this time, it was not salty sad tears. They were literally tears with a sweetness to them when they fell upon my upper lip. Tears of a most massive gratitude for an immeasurably beautiful gift. What an absolute treasure to have shared that one evening with such a family.

Alberto and his family represent TRUE WEALTH. They have never left my heart and never will.

* * *

Epilogue:

My personal sense of wealth began to take shape that day—years ago in Mexico.

It was the 'tipping point' on the scale, for the WEIGHT of TRUE WORTH in life.

If you've allowed yourself to read this far—you most certainly have humanitarian ideals within.

You see that lasting happiness can't find a foothold on a base of sensation-seeking.

So then, the gift of living –of being human– isn't it <u>REAL</u>-LY about the freedoms we each have to make choices that FIT US?!

Life is ultimately about learning & growing right? So, no matter what lifestyle you live—chosen or not...it is safe to say there will always be harsh lessons during different periods along the way.

Fact of Life.

We all can likely agree from our own unique, yet deeply challenging personal experiences.

So why not move forward in life now, with a new perspective inspired by Alberto.

Grow into FEELING a life of great value.

Try to live more contently in this present moment, observing your own feelings.

HOW?

Advice is one thing that is freely given away.
Be watchful you only take that which is worth having.
~George S. Clason

I hope if this story even resonates a little— the following will be advice worth implementing for greater riches, value and wealth in your life. Because life is too short not to question. It's too short not to try new ways of thinking for yourself—thinking differently than the masses—questioning societal values put upon you or your children.

Maybe it starts with removing activities, things and even people (sadly enough) you thought you needed–but which and who don't jive deep down with you and your own personal sense of what's valuable in life.

If something causes you to lose your sense of peace, or feel unsettled –it may be your sign– that the time has come to de-clutter a particular aspect of your life and usher in a shift in lifestyle.

De-cluttering life of unnecessary stresses, when we all have plenty that must be dealt with anyway...will open doors to pursuing things & people that/who you may have neglected to even see before.

So, try to take some quiet moments and examine what would allow you to feel a greater sense of freedom in the ways Alberto felt it. What can be removed that was brought into your life by social constraints, or what you were taught to believe you SHOULD do?

Allow time focused on small wealthier moments, full of peace because of their connectedness with authentic values. Discover how the small moments and the little things in life are often more significant and hold more meaning to the heart's core—as well as to our personal growth.

If you would be a real seeker after truth, it is necessary that at least once in your life you doubt all things.
~Rene Descartes

WEALTH– finding those activities you love and making the time to do them more often, even when it means setting aside what society would consider more important. It is understanding oneself enough to sense what is disingenuous and know how do disengage.

WEALTH– realizing that pleasing others at your own expense is not going to help anyone in the end. This benefits family as well because you know your children will follow a path of being true to themselves and gain those feelings of true wealth (like Alberto had)…in the process.

WEALTH– relishing the moments you are able

to connect authentically and deeply with another; knowing that these moments are sometimes few and far between. It is realizing that they are therefore a precious treasure to be cherished and valued.

WEALTH– the act of going out of one's way to do some small kindness that could potentially mean the world to another.

WEALTH– making time to talk, read or create something with a loved one; it is learning something new…it is journal writing, heart-to-heart talks over a meal; it is a quiet walk amongst nature, unexpected moments of laughter, time with our pets, intellectual conversations with those we admire, dancing to good music, a hot bath, watching the snow fall….

When one feels "un-wealthy" in life for reasons any number of people would agree were valid… I hope they have someone like Alberto and his children to remember.

It can take you right out of selfish thinking and straight into leading a life of TRUE WEALTH.

Soon, the un-wealthy feelings are replaced with a sense of peace and GRATITUDE!

Here's to Finding your True Wealth.

* * *

~ The Beginning ~

If you enjoyed this story, please take a moment to submit an honest review on Amazon.

Your effort to do this might allow someone else to consider reading it and maybe, possibly help in some way.

Thank you for reading.

Made in the USA
Middletown, DE
27 October 2022